To Harold Simons.
with all good wishes,

Paul Hahn

TROUBLE SHOTS

PAUL HAHN

Shows You
How to Play
TROUBLE
SHOTS

ILLUSTRATED by LEA GUSTAVSON

DAVID McKAY COMPANY, Inc.   NEW YORK

PAUL HAHN SHOWS YOU HOW TO PLAY
TROUBLE SHOTS

Illustrated by Lea Gustavson

LIBRARY OF CONGRESS CATALOG CARD NUMBER: 65-13139

MANUFACTURED IN THE UNITED STATES OF AMERICA

VAN REES PRESS   •   NEW YORK

DEDICATION

As a young caddy I was inspired to become a golf professional by our local country club professional, Henry Picard. Both Picard and Johnny Adams (pro at our hometown municipal golf course where I caddied) were great stylists and I was among four youngsters who turned pro because of these two gentlemen. Picard became a national figure and I tried to emulate his golf powers.

Bob Hope gave me a big boost with reams of comedy material, much of which I still use today.

To these three who engendered so much initiative, I dedicate this book.

INTRODUCTION

by Arnold Palmer

IF THERE WAS EVER a golf professional versed in the lore of trouble shots and their execution, it is Paul Hahn.

Paul seems to have the grasp on shot making in any given situation.

His exhibitions prove his ability to execute seemingly impossible shots and his clear presentation should prove invaluable to all who read his concise counsel.

TABLE OF CONTENTS

FOREWORD

Whenever the odd shot confronts you, you should simply ask yourself:

How do I play this shot? In the following pages you will see illustrations and written suggestions that easily solve the problem.

Why should I play it this way instead of another way? This question is reasonable and logical. It will be answered in these pages with analytical copy and illustrations.

When and where does the condition arise that necessitates my playing the shot this way? Throughout this book you will find problem shots and solutions. Some shots require alternate solutions. All factors are considered and explained.

What result can I expect from this shot? No one, really no one, expects miracles. However, we give an excellent appraisal of your can-do and cannot do. We also illustrate and advise you so that you will be completely realistic about what you can expect and about the margins for error strewn all along the path. We will weigh each problem for you, give you the possible solution, and then tell you what you should expect for your efforts.

BASIC PHILOSOPHY

THE ABILITY to shave many strokes off your golf score may be far simpler than you realize. So-called trouble shots in golf can become much easier to execute if the golfer stores in his brain the fact that there are devious ways to hit the ball and turn a potential triple-bogey into a par and even a birdie.

Consider that there is no rule that precludes one's turning the clubface on end and hitting the ball with the opposite stroke. Consider, too, that no rule in the book says one must hit from an orthodox stance or position the ball at any given point, relative to the line of flight. The tournament champions know this; many have had to curve a ball out of bounds for many yards and still have the ball return to fair territory. This is but one example of how one may save strokes. In the ensuing chapters and illustrations you will readily see how great is the reward for merely thinking of alternate ways to extricate yourself from a potential missed shot.

In my exhibition routine I have been called on to hit many unorthodox shots with regular clubs and vice versa. This has taken a considerable amount of practice time. However, who is so unrealistic as to think any game can be mastered without devoting a liberal amount of time to getting a muscular groove and development and add to this a keen sense of timing.

The vicious cycle will become your teammate when you decide to practice until you become reasonably proficient. From this practice possible. Now look at the sketch of the right hand turned to the right. The position shown indicates that the right hand, being stronger than the left, will return to its normal position during the swing and close the left, turning it back counterclockwise.

For an intentional hook, this is good positioning. Turning the left hand to the right at the same time almost insures a hook.

For an intentional fade, the opposite is the case. Of course we assume that all other things are equal, i.e., the proper stance, balance, and swing.

THE GRIP

OVERLAP OR
VARDON GRIP

THE MOST popular grip in use in the world today is the overlapping grip. It is popular because it is the most functional type.

The clubshaft is extended diagonally across the lower part of the left palm and the upper part of the fingers of the left hand. When closed, the last three digits hold the club firmly against the butt-pad of the palm. This is the firmest part of the human hand. Hold firmly but not tightly.

The inverted "V" formed by the thumb and forefinger should point in the general direction of the right shoulder. Strong players have their "V" pointing more to the chin than would average players. The thumb is placed a quarter of the way around the shaft for the average golfer. Tournament players usually put the thumb on the top of the shaft to preclude wildly hooking shots. Three knuckles should be visible when looking straight down. This, too, is for average players; top golf stars have only one or two knuckles visible.

In the right hand the club is placed in the second knuckle joint of the middle three fingers. It is hard to get a beginner to hold the club this way. Most golfers try to choke the club to death in the knuckle joint near the palm. This will put the right hand under the shaft and render it useless in performing its proper function. Close the right hand over the left thumb and turn it to the left if necessary for the right thumb to be a quarter of the way around the left side of the shaft. The inverted "V" formed by the thumb and forefinger of the right hand should also point in the general direction of the right shoulder or slightly to the left of it.

Getting used to the proper grip will take time, but patience will pay off in good golf shots.

THE GRIP:
NORMAL, WEAK, AND STRONG

Since we transmit both power and control through the hands, it would be folly indeed to consider anything but a good grip. It is the only connection between the animate golfer and the inanimate club, which contacts the ball. A golfer with a poor grip must set up compensations to overcome the defective action that will be produced. The factor of the wrist function is two-sided. If you use a powerful grip, you may wreak havoc with a shot; with a weak grip you may lessen your chances of getting great distances.

To hit a curving ball to the right, as in a fade or a slice, it is wise

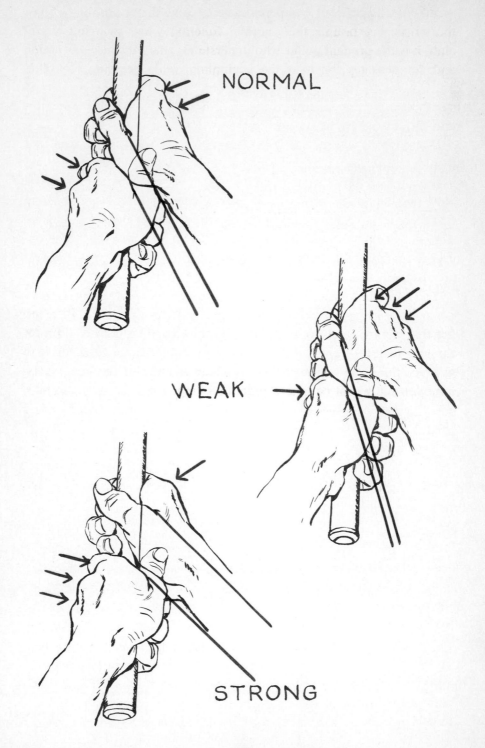

NORMAL

WEAK

STRONG

to place the hands more counterclockwise on the shaft of the club. Since the wrists will resume their normal function when swinging a golf club, it is the prudent golfer who understands this subconscious action and compensates for it at the beginning, while gripping the club. For a curve to the left we use the strong grip. The hands are turned clockwise on the shaft so that the right hand will subconsciously turn into a hooking pronation during the swing.

When would you try this type of grip? On the practice tee first, and then only when you need a curving shot. At all other times you should use a normal, conventional grip. While the overlapping grip is the most popular today, professional golfers have found and are teaching that there is no disadvantage in using a full-finger or interlocking grip. The placement of the hands on the club shaft will find the wrists opposing each other as in the overlapping grip. This type grip is recommended only for people with small or weak hands.

The most important part of learning to grip the club properly is to make certain right from the start that you will have patience. Remember that we are creatures of habit. It takes a good amount of time for the grip to feel "right," and an even longer amount of time for it to produce the shots you expect of it. Make a study of the hands each time you hit a shot or take a practice swing. Soon you will discover that the new grip begins to feel "right," and the old one will feel strange.

EXTREME HAND POSITIONS

THERE ARE extreme positions for the wrists that render the grip as ineffective as it was effective in the illustration shown. Consider the fact that each hand can move in any of four directions by merely moving it at the wrist. The wrists have two hinges: up and down and sideways, left or right. When we turn either hand beyond 45 degrees we allow the sideways movement to take command of the action. In the illustration shown, the wrists have gone through every possible turn. This shows very clearly that we should consider just what type of shot should be played for each situation and adjust the grip accordingly. Let the subconscious movements of the wrists do the work; they will.

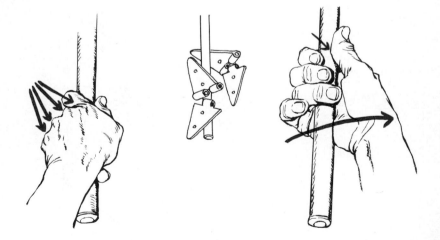

OVER-EXAGGERATED STRONG GRIP, IN
EITHER OR BOTH HANDS BECOMES **WEAK**

PLAYING THE PICCOLO

IT IS far easier to let the club go at the top of the swing than it is to hold on firmly. That is why so very many golfers find themselves "playing the piccolo," as illustrated here.

A simple exercise can help overcome this very normal mistake. Remember that it will take a little time to get used to the "funny" feeling we get from making a change. Hold the club firmly and swing up to the top of the swing. Repeat this at least ten times before you try hitting a ball. Of course you wouldn't want to do this while playing a round of golf, for you would be holding up the parade. But do try it on the practice tee, in your office, or in your backyard or living room. In time you will find it not so uncomfortable to hold on to the club firmly

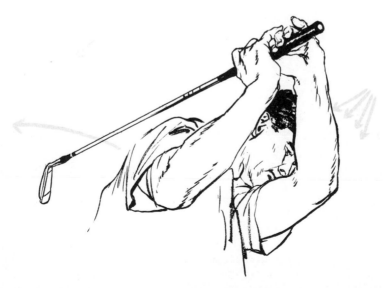

at the top of the swing, and your reward will be some crisply hit shots that mean lower scores for you.

The grip is too important a factor to let this go unnoticed. You should understand that if you let the club go loose at the top of the swing it will have to be regripped somewhere in the downswing. This will mean that your rhythm pattern has been broken and the tempo of your swing lost, and a missed shot will usually be your sad fate.

Your muscles and tendons will stretch for this. They will soon adapt to this new feel, and you will be a far happier golfer.

ANGLE OF ATTACK, PLANE, AND BALANCE

ASSUMING that the golfer has learned how to hold the club properly and how to stand up to the ball, we need stress only that the angle at which the clubface strikes the ball will be the determining factor in just how the ball will fly.

Since golf is contrary to natural instinct, it is imperative that one learns to hit the opposite from what he thinks the angle should be. By this we mean if you want a ball to curve to the right you hit across it to the left. By the same token, should you desire a curve to the left, you merely hit across the ball to the right. The same goes for hitting a ball high into the air. The clubface must descend on the ball in a fast downstroke with plenty of wrist action. For the low shot into the wind, you must play the ball back toward the rear foot and drag the club through the shot with as little wrist action as possible.

The plane of the swing will usually be determined by the height

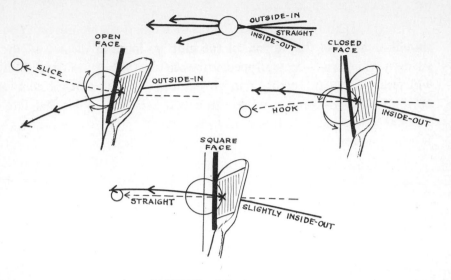

ANGLES OF ATTACK

of the player. Suffice it to say that a short person will normally have a flatter plane (see plane and arc, page 46) and the taller person an upright swing.

The balance factor cannot be stressed too strongly. In golf there is one point to consider when addressing the ball for regular shots: make certain you can turn away from the ball and back into the shot with no restrictions. Sit down to the ball much the same as a rider would do on a horse. Flexing the knees is a prime requisite for all shots, with the possible exception of the putter (but then most good putters have their knees flexed even more because they are stooped over due to the short length of the putter shaft).

Since the grip is the only actual connection between the golfer and the golf club, it stands to reason that the hands should be placed on the club so that the wrist action will bring the proper motion through each shot. Slight adjustments can help in turning the ball in a hook or slice curve.

SPIN OF THE BALL

Too few golfers realize that it is almost impossible to put any great amount of backspin on a very short pitch or chip shot. They see the top tournament player hit shots to the green that bounce once or twice and spin backward. What they do not realize is that the shot was hit from a distance farther out. The backspin is produced by a descending clubface on the ball, with no grass or oily substance between the clubface and ball to eliminate the friction that causes the spin. The greater the velocity of the stroke, the greater the spin; the sharper the angle of attack, the greater the spin.

When a good player is faced with a short shot that must have some stopping action on the ball, because of the size of the green or some other factor, the most proficient players use what they call the "flip-shot," which is done with an open clubface, played off the left foot,

BACKSPIN

LITTLE OR NO SPIN

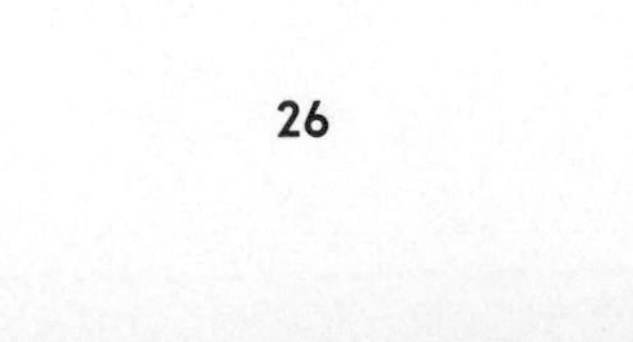

TOPPED OVERSPIN

and with extensive use of the wrists. This is a delicate shot, a soft shot. The ball does stop in a reasonably short distance, but because of the *angle* of the trajectory, not backspin.

Since this type of shot requires many hours of practice, it would be wise to consider how much you have to put in the practice-bank to be able to make an occasional withdrawal.

THINK ALTERNATE ROUTE

No MATTER how many rounds of golf you play, you will never see the day when all your drives go straight down the fairway or all your irons wind up on the green and your putts drop. This is axiomatic. How wise, though, is the golfer who has his mind keyed to thinking of how to score despite these errant shots. Most of the old-time money winners were terrific "scramblers." In fact, several won the Open and the PGA Championship.

There is no rule that says you must play each shot in the same manner as the last. If you merely think of an alternate route every time you are faced with a difficult shot, you will have the edge over practically every other golfer. Far too few ever consider hitting the ball against a building or wall to make it carom back into the fair territory. There are hundreds of ways to find shots that are not "normal" but ones that would cut strokes from your score. Angle the face of your club, stand at an obtuse angle, hit the ball with the back of the clubface—all of these things are legal and can save you strokes. The prize goes to the one who can score well, and smart thinking can definitely improve your scores.

Many situations arise in a daily round of golf where a curving arc is more desirable than a straight ball. Around a dog-leg hole's fairway, around an obstacle, even curving it out of bounds for some distance and back into fair territory can be the shot necessary to place the ball in position for the subsequent shot. When would you do this? Any time the wind condition permits, assuming, of course, that the club selected can give the desired trajectory and distance.

The ability to make a golf shot curve either to the left or right should not be a talent limited to tournament players. It is one kind of shot that can be executed by any fairly good player.

Consider first the angle of attack. Consider, too, that the clubface must cross the ball at an angle opposite the intended line of flight. Remember that for a curving shot low into the wind, you must play the ball back towards the center of the stance and restrict the wrist action through the hitting area. For a high shot, you must play the ball off the left foot and use plenty of wrist action. If greater height or lower trajectory is called for, shift your body balance back toward your right foot for height or forward onto your left foot for a low ball. Concentrate on keeping a steady head position; the most common fault of the average golfer is to move away from the ball in an attempt to curve the ball with "body action." Extreme boldness is absolutely necessary in making this shot effective. Confidence may be enhanced by a few practice shots of the kind mentioned above.

THE STANCES:
OPEN, SQUARE, AND CLOSED

ONE OF THE most important factors contributing to the direction a golf ball will travel is the stance. A golfer aims and balances with his feet. There are three types of stances for three distinct types of shots. In all three, the knees should be flexed for better balance.

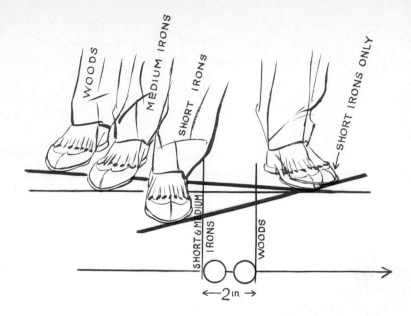

The open stance is for the shots ranging from the number five iron down to the wedge. The stance is just slightly open for the number five iron and graduates more and more open until it is very wide open for the number nine iron and the two wedges, the pitching wedge and the sand wedge. The purpose of using an open stance is to make the clubhead travel naturally outside the line in the backswing (see illustration) and return down across the line in the downswing. This action produces a "cut" across the ball, which in turn creates a spin that will hold the ball when it hits the green.

The square stance is for all shots in the medium and long range. If greater distance is desired, the square stance may be a bit wider than the distance between the shoulders of an average-sized person. This is a standard measurement—square stance about shoulder width. The feet should be turned slightly outward. This allows better balance and footwork.

The closed stance is one used for hitting the drive and most fully extended shots. It is also used for intentionally hooking a ball. The right foot is withdrawn from the line (see illustration) to allow a full turn of the shoulders and a half turn of the torso. Distance comes from this wide turn. This type of stance promotes the action from in-

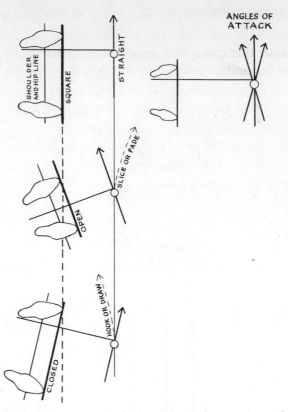

side out in the impact area and should produce a long hooking arc. The hook in itself produces more distance. It is wise, however, to consider how difficult it is to control a hooked shot. Be certain to keep the head steady for all shots.

THE BALANCE FACTOR, THE BIG FACTOR

Too OFTEN overlooked in considering things fundamental to good golf is the one precipitator of composure—balance. This is so manifest in the swings of all good golfers that it is amazing how few realize its importance. With the new power hitters making headlines and cash, balance becomes an even greater must.

First, consider that controlled speed is the essence of good golf; then consider how incredibly precise a good shot must be. How then can we justify any attempt to hit a golf shot without good balance? Countless golfers try to imitate the motions made by the greats of the links. In their intrepretation they lose sight of the key factors involved. The weight distribution is the first to be considered. With the weight forward on the toes it is impossible to hit a good golf shot. The weight must be evenly distributed between the two feet and back towards

the heel. For shorter iron shots the weight is distributed with a bit more on the left foot than the right. This minimizes the actual shifting of weight that in short shots produces a margin for error.

Study the illustration of the tremendous turn of the shoulders and torso in the backswing. This is actually the windup or backstretch. Then note how well balanced the weight is, shifted back into hitting position and on through the ball up to a good high finish.

The width of the stance can affect the balance factor. Too narrow a stance will usually produce an off-balance swing. With too wide a stance you will have little possibility of shifting the weight, as is done in the golf swing's pivot.

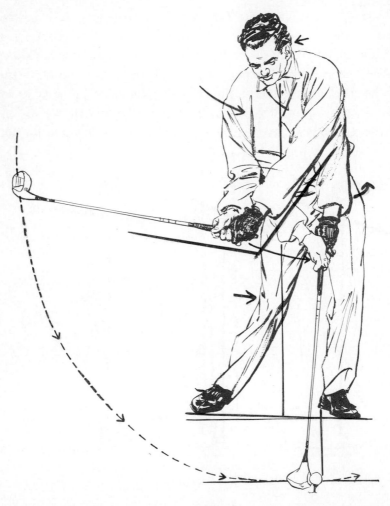

THE RIGHT AND WRONG
OF WEIGHT SHIFTING

FIRE AND fall back. This action is more manifest on the golf course today because the new breed of tournament player stresses distance and power. When the novice tries to get power into a golf shot, he must use what force he has—the thigh and torso muscles. Invariably he will lean into the shot in the backswing and fall away from it on the downswing, which falls in line with Newton's theory of action-reaction. Today's players keep the left heel fairly low and do not

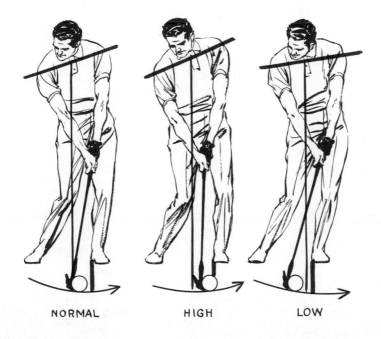

NORMAL   HIGH   LOW

lift it like the players of a generation ago. They have found that they can turn their shoulders to describe the arc and reduce the margin for error, while delivering at the proper time all the power they can muster.

Good balance is a prime requisite. In the correct illustration note that the head and shoulders have stayed over the balance point while the weight has shifted to the left along the line of intended flight.

The illustration on the right shows how the club will hit the ball in its ascent and therefore top the shot. This usually happens when the golfer *tries* to elevate the shot. Depend on the loft of the club and your downward stroke to get the ball into the air. This is the only way it can be done.

Your composure will be more like that of the champion after you develop the "golf" muscles the champions have. Making continual changes can only create more confusion. Stay with the procedure your professional recommends for you, practice assiduously, and your reward will be many great shots and greater satisfaction.

POWER UNDER CONTROL

To TRANSFER the weight on the hips, to turn away from the
address position and return to the ball, requires a type of composure
needed in no other sport.

The tremendous force generated by the body turn, the arms swinging
and the wrists unleashing their power, can be a source of misses. But
to harness this power and put the right amount in at the right time is
the answer to most long-shot problems.

The illustration shows a golfer with a plumb line hanging down from the front of the collar. In actuality you could use precisely this method. However, it will serve your purpose just as well merely to imagine its being there. In action, this shows that the center of the swing is being maintained even though all the motion of the shoulders and hips is in a state of constant flux.

To appreciate this fully, close your eyes and visualize how this plumb-line theory works. The head and shoulders form the center of the golf swing. A steady head is indicative of all good golfers. Note that while the shoulders turn to describe the arc, they turn directly over the balance point. This is the axis of the arc. To move this axis off-center except for intentional variances is to create a margin for error that can, and usually does, cause many missed shots.

CONTROLLED SPEED— POINT OF POWER

IF ALL the golfers of the world would harness their energy in their golf swing and apply it at the precise time, there would be little need for instructions. There are two basic factors in golf, position and action. Anyone can learn the proper positions simply by taking lessons and studying the grip and stance (as shown in this book) until they become second nature. But the big fault-factor is action, for here is where we must control our primitive urge to knock the cover off the ball.

If you can put the steam in at the right point, the point of power, you have taken a big step in the right direction. The super-fast backswing is almost always a kiss of death to the golfer. Few have ever learned to control a fast backswing. The only way to overcome this is to think, consciously think, of smoothness. Worry not about the speed, just think of smoothness, and you'll discover that your sympathetic nervous system will give you a slower backswing. Think, too, of the backswing as a stretching windup, and let your ear detect the big swish as the clubface enters the hitting area.

A common fault is to try to slow down a fast backswing by making the motion so slow and deliberate that tension creeps in and removes any possibility of a well-coordinated shot. If you can stop your backswing at your predetermined point, and be in balance and control, your backswing is not too fast. Think smooth, not slow. Think smoothness throughout your entire swing, and you will soon discover the thrill of controlled speed—which is actually only good timing.

THE ADDRESS

QUITE POSSIBLY the most overlooked fundamental in golf is the address. This little motion, a wiggle or waggle, made over the ball before the swing is started does two things of great importance.

First, it gets the golfer acquainted with the feel of the clubhead. All good golfers predicate their good shots on feel.

Second, and more important, the address prepares the golfer mentally, and removes the tension precipitated by thinking of the multitude of things he feels he should be thinking about before swinging the club. Mind and muscle coordination is practically impossible when tension ties up the golf swing.

Watch the composed swings of good golfers, and you'll see them address the ball first and then let fly that smoothly hit shot. Confidence comes from being sure of oneself. Confidence can be yours much more easily if you will address the ball before taking your backswing.

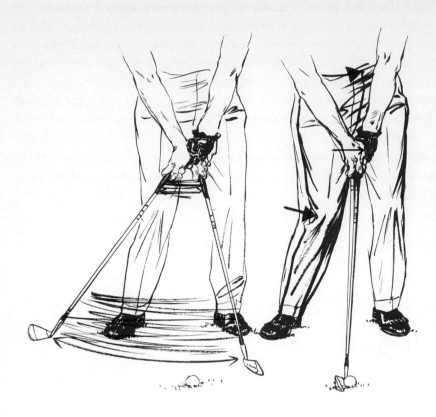

WAGGLE   FORWARD PRESS

THE FORWARD PRESS

STUDY CLOSELY the mannerisms of the great professional golfers, either in person or on television, and you may note a peculiar motion made by all of them just prior to taking the club back. Just as they finish their address they kink in their knee toward the line of flight. Some also do it with the hands. Sam Snead has the most obvious "forward press" in pro golf.

This forward press is made to get the swing started smoothly. It sets the swing in motion without creating a margin for error. If you have ever hit a foreign object or irregular grass in the initial part of your backswing you probably remember that you lost your sense of rhythm and missed or half-hit the shot. It is extremely difficult to keep up the rhythm pattern of your swing if it is interrupted. When rhythm is broken, the cycle of your swing is broken, and you usually hasten the swing. Results? Disaster!

Understand the purpose of the "forward press," and you will be happy to include it in your backswing. It does help the top pros; it can help you.

THE BACKSWING

ONE OF THE questions most often asked touring professionals and pros who give golf clinics is, "How do you start the backswing?" One thing is certain—good golfers start everything together. Sometimes it is necessary for a club professional to advise starting with the hands, with the shoulders, with the pivot, or with the arms. In so doing, he makes you exaggerate one move in order to preclude a wrong one. This is compensatory.

The proper way to start the golf swing is by thinking of the backswing as one big assembly. Everything goes back together. Straight back, arms, hands, clubhead; everything turns away from the ball, slightly inside the line as the shoulders turn to describe the arc. Make certain the head and shoulders stay over the ball, the head steady, the shoulders turning. The left shoulder goes under the chin in the backswing.

Stretch back fully for your long shots. This fully extended back-swing will enable you to muster your greatest forces for full delivery of power at impact.

The greatest must in the backswing is to be as unhurried as possible. The tempo of your swing is determined in the backswing. If you snatch the club back too fast, the immediate reaction is to hit from the top of the swing. Taking the club back smoothly will enable you to get full thrust in the downswing.

You have reached the top of your backswing when your left arm starts to bend at the elbow and the hands start to lose their grip on the club.

THE CRITICAL POINT
IN THE GOLF SWING

EVERY ACTION that requires precision has a critical point, and the most critical point in the golf swing is unquestionably the first move in the downswing. This is the point that separates all the men from all the boys. Getting up to the top of the swing should present no great problem: merely take everything back together—hands, arms, shoulder turn, clubhead, and weight shift.

But at the top of the swing the great majority of golfers try to hit the ball with every ounce of power they can muster. Typical is the lunge we see so often. Also typical is the right shoulder turning over the ball and causing a wide slicing arc. It is a very human reaction—black out mentally, hit the ball as hard as possible, and hope and pray for the best.

It takes practice to master the correct beginning of the downswing. Return the weight to the left side, on the hips. Get set for hitting the shot by having good balance and a delay of the wrist action. The only way to accomplish this is to have a "positive" move at the outset. Make certain that you shift the weight back to the left side first, and you may be amazed to see that your wrists are still fully cocked over halfway down in the downswing. You'll find the positive move of the hips at the start of the downswing has caused the arms and hands to drop into hitting position with no conscious effort on your part. Note in the illustrations how this works. Remember that it is contrary to every natural instinct; naturally you want to hit the ball hard. You cannot do it by thinking of what *not* to do; your every thought should be of smoothness throughout the swing. By returning the weight to the left side as the first move in the downswing, you naturally get into hitting position with no effort. Then the acceleration of power brings about that long shot you have hoped for. Some good golfers find that twisting their hips serves the same purpose, but this is highly individual and should not be attempted by the average golfer.

ONE-ARM PRACTICE

For most right-handed golfers the left arm is the weaker and the right arm the stronger. Since the left arm is the guiding element throughout the entire swing, shouldn't the left side be somewhat stronger than it is?

Many good golfers begin the season by strengthening the left side with a one-arm practice. In the illustration shown on page 42 the left arm alone is swinging the club. I have taught this for years and am one of many professionals who show golfers how simple it is to ac-

centuate the positive by strengthening it. Lack of action in the right side serves to equalize the natural difference in strength.

It is definitely not an easy thing to do. At first you will be fortunate if your left arm, kept straight, is strong enough to lift the club up to your waist. But in time you will definitely increase your capacity, and soon you can describe a full swing with just your left arm and forearm. Keep this side strong by continually practicing this exercise, and you will be hitting much better golf shots.

The second illustration shows the golfer finishing the swing with only the left hand on the club. Here he has taken the club back with both hands and actually hit at the ball with both hands and then let the right hand leave the shaft at impact. Many very capable golf instructors have taught this for years in an attempt to cure the common slice. It has worked in most every case. The tough part is to make students continue practicing. This they must do.

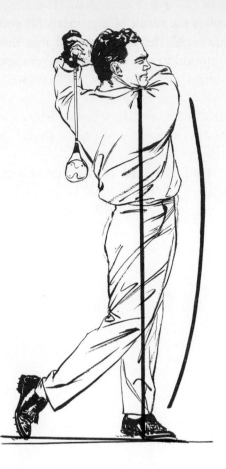

THE FOLLOW-THROUGH

Oɴᴇ ᴘᴀʀᴛ of the golf swing that is often posed is the
follow-through. Let us look at it honestly; there are many ways to hit
out a fairly respectable golf shot. But invariably a golfer who hits with

a poor swing will raise his hands in a salute follow-through as if to indicate that he had made a perfect shot. He is only kidding himself.

A follow-through is the result of a properly hit golf shot. When you consciously hit "through" the shot you will find the momentum will carry you up and around to a beautiful finish, graceful and high. Note in the illustration the arch of the body, the arms and hands held high. This is a study of force and composure. The force has been expended, but we note its result in making the body arch and the club finish high. Note, too, how well composed and balanced the golfer looks. This is the essence of the follow-through.

Swing properly from the start of the downswing and the follow-through will be right. Never fake a good follow-through. It only makes you look slightly ridiculous and doesn't help your golf progress one bit.

THE PLANE OF THE SWING

YOUR PHYSICAL structure determines the plane of your swing. Ordinarily a tall person will have an upright swing and a short person a flat swing. However, this does not always hold true. Many big, tall people are "locking up" their swings by taking the club back in a flat plane and keeping the clubface completely closed. This produces a hook on almost every shot, except when the player has turned both hands counterclockwise to a weak position, to make the hands turn the clubface square at impact.

The best course is to take the club straight back from the ball and let your individual physique determine which is best for you. At the Masters in Augusta, during my first appearance there, I studied very closely the distinctive swing of the inimitable Ben Hogan. He is a bit shorter than my six-feet-one, but his perfect control of all shots made me study very hard my chances of flattening the plane of my swing. I worked for several years on locking up my backswing for control and had it working fairly well in most instances. However, when I forget the unique grip (weak) that must be used, I fly the ball into the left rough or out of bounds every time.

Reach straight back (as seen in the upright illustration) and, if you are short, you will still have a somewhat flatter swing than a tall person. Extend your arc and your plane will almost fit into a groove consistent with your physical type.

It is a proved fact that the more upright the swing, the easier it is to hit a straight ball. The club ascending and descending from straight

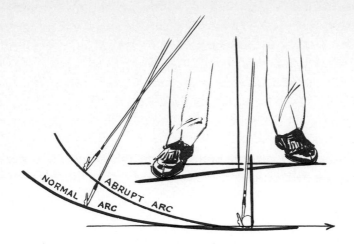

behind the ball will certainly produce more straight shots than a clubhead wheeling in from inside out. From a flat plane there is infinitely more accuracy and adroitness required, for the clubface is square to the line for only a split second. Stick to the swing that fits your physique and eliminate the hours of hard work that you'll need to compensate for the bad effects caused by attempting anything else.

THE UPRIGHT AND NORMAL PLANE

Too OFTEN a golfer finds his shot slicing or hooking off the fairway and into the rough. Sometimes this rough can be fairly high, and trouble to get out of.

For a shot from high grass we suggest you know something about the plane and the arc of the swing. There are three regular types of plane: the flat, the normal, and the upright. The flatter the plane the more the ball will be compressed at impact, velocity being equal.

Sometimes, however, distance must be sacrificed, and an upright plane is the only one that will get the ball extricated from the rough. The clubhead must descend just behind the ball and leave as little foreign matter between the clubface and the ball as possible.

Distance can be obtained by playing the upright plane and the ball off the right foot, but often you will have a tendency to top the ball in this type of shot. Off the left foot the ball will rise swiftly and, while you might lose some distance, you will get the ball out of the rough.

From heavy grass it will be folly to try to hit through the grass. The ball would never go straight toward the object since the grass would cushion the stroke, and the grass is seldom, if ever, as smooth or as straight as a clubface. Add to this the oily substance in all grass that would take away the spin and you have double trouble.

HIGH, NORMAL, AND LOW SHOTS

THE PROFICIENT player finds himself faced with shots that require more or less than normal trajectory. You will note from the three drawings here that in the normal shot the weight is evenly balanced on the hips and the head and shoulders stay back of the ball. The hands are in the proper position for this shot of normal trajectory.

For the high trajectory shift the weight back toward the right foot but maintain good balance and hit the ball with as much action as

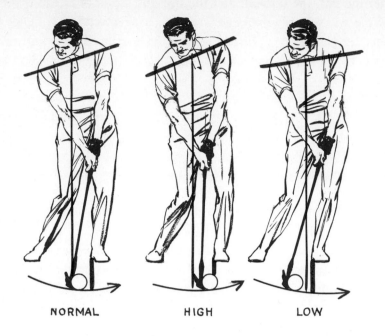

NORMAL   HIGH   LOW

is possible, playing the ball slightly forward of the left heel position.

Conversely, for a low shot you would lean slightly into the ball (shifting the weight forward) toward the line of flight, restricting the wrist action through the ball and playing the ball back towards the center of the stance. This shot can be very effective when playing in windy conditions.

It would be unwise to try any of these shots 'until you have had many sessions on the practice tee.

POSITION FOR HITTING
THE DRIVE AND LONG WOODS

Note in the illustration that a fairly wide nonrestrictive stance is used to allow a full turn and at the same time not hinder balance. One great source of power is the turn of the shoulders. When using this technique, be sure to consider the balance factor. This can be done more easily if you are sitting down to the ball, as noted from the sketch of the sideview. Note that the flexed knees allow a complete turn away from the ball and that returning the weight to the left side gives one the necessary power to propel the clubhead to the ball at its greatest possible velocity. Remember, velocity squared by weight equals distance. But also remember that clubhead speed is more important than weight.

Too wide a stance causes a restricted shoulder turn. Too narrow a stance creates the possibility of losing balance. Usually a stance slightly wider than shoulder width will produce your best shots with the longest clubs, the woods.

The slightly closed stance allows a far greater turn away from the ball, and the long arc produces infinitely more distance. You'll find a tendency to hook the ball with a closed stance, but a slight adjustment of your grip will keep the ball in the fairway. This was the Ben Hogan system for precluding the duck-hook. Just turn the left hand slightly counterclockwise and the right hand a bit in the same direction to a weak grip position.

Note the position of the hands. This is higher than at any other time. A full extension is necessary to make the fullest turn, and the high hand position must be considered. There is a slight kink downward but certainly not as it is in the irons.

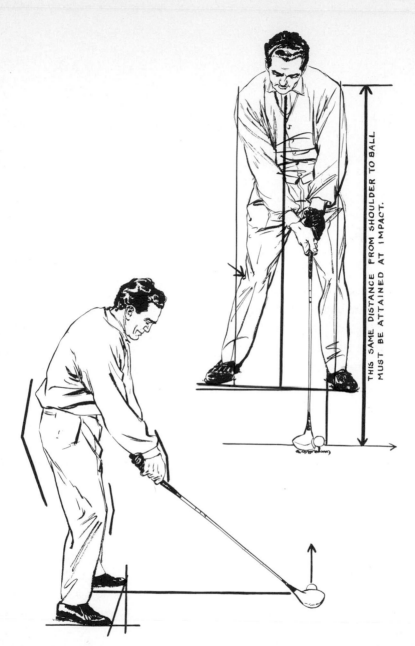

THIS SAME DISTANCE FROM SHOULDER TO BALL MUST BE ATTAINED AT IMPACT.

Note that the ball is played as far away as is comfortable to reach. Too close a position would cramp the swing; too far away would force the player to reach for the ball and lose precious balance in so doing. Remember the word composure and let it always be in your thinking when executing long golf shots. It is the mark of the champion.

51

THE TEE SHOT

From time to time you will be faced with the decision of teeing the ball high or low. Several things can assist you in making the tee shot work better for you. First, consider the angle of attack. If you are hitting against the wind, it would be far better to tee the ball up as high as practicable and play the ball a bit towards the center of the stance. If you hit with less wrist than normal, the ball will have less backspin and consequently climb less. Conversely, when faced with a wind shot that makes a high shot desirable, tee the ball lower so that you may hit down on the ball, giving the shot extra backspin and sending it up fast. You are also less likely to hook. Another way to make a high shot is to hit off a high tee and fly the ball into the air with full power and no loss from more backspin.

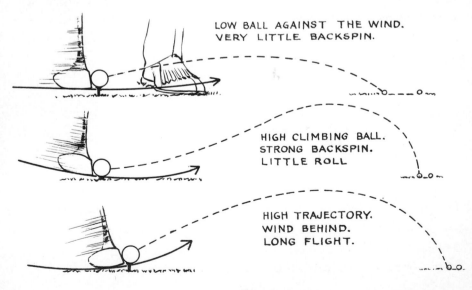

LOW BALL AGAINST THE WIND.
VERY LITTLE BACKSPIN.

HIGH CLIMBING BALL.
STRONG BACKSPIN.
LITTLE ROLL

HIGH TRAJECTORY.
WIND BEHIND.
LONG FLIGHT.

THE BASER INSTINCT

THERE ARE two schools of thought on how to tee the drive when an out-of-bounds line parallels the fairway. One school prescribes a hit out towards the boundary, assuming that the golfer will let the clubface cross the ball at that angle, which will, in effect, curve the ball away from the forbidden land.

However, considering the instinctiveness with which most golfers avoid the two-stroke penalty country, we note the advisability of teeing the drive on the out-of-bounds side and hitting away from the trouble. This applies to any other situation in which an obstruction could prove a nightmare to your golf score.

If you tee your drive near the boundary side, you will hit either a straight ball or a pulled shot since your instinct will not allow the folly of your hitting out toward the farmer's pasture. The angle at which the ball will be struck will insure you a safe shot, unless, of course, you grip and swing so badly that not even your Blue Cross could save you.

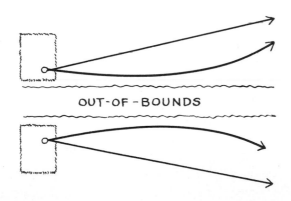

OUT-OF-BOUNDS

FAIRWAY WOODS

For most golfers the fairway wood shots are the toughest to hit properly. This is due primarily to the fact that most golfers try to elevate the ball by leaning back and hitting up on the ball. This is the height of disaster. Falling away is a most common error, as the average golfer will try to lift the ball out of a close lie with body English. Think of the angle of attack: if you hit down on the ball, it will rise; if you hit up on the ball, it will be half-hit or topped. More often than not, the club will strike the turf before the ball. Hitting behind the ball seems to be a very common shot on the fairways of the world.

Try a slightly descending sweeping stroke off the fairways. If the ball is on a slope, below the feet, hit to the left, as you will probably fade the ball. Should the ball be on a sidehill above your feet, aim to the right, as the ball will hook. In a tight lie on the fairway, make certain the downward stroke is more profound. But at all times, hit through the shot.

Firm wrists and hand action will bring better fairway wood shots for everyone, especially when the lie is poor. If the clubface cannot be soled behind the ball it might be wise to consider another club, rather than a wood. Some situations demand that you relinquish distance, and this is tough to take. Some golfers will take a wood even though they know they must miss the shot. And, believe me, they will.

The inconsiderate golfer who fails to replace his divot will always provide a tough lie for anyone finding his ball in this divot hole. But hitting fairway woods from some divot holes can be done if you consider these simple facts: composure, firm grip, angle of attack, and hitting through the shot. You'll find fairway woods not so difficult as you thought.

USING WOODS FROM THE ROUGH

I T IS extremely foolish for a golfer to select a wood for anything other than a perfect lie in the rough. The chances of his hitting a good shot are almost negligible. It is tantamount to reaching into a barrel of deadly snakes and hoping to pull out an eel.

Few of the golfing greats on a professional tour would dare use a wood from the rough unless the ball were sitting up or on a good lie. Unless contact can be made with the ball first, with no grass between the clubface and the ball, there is little hope for a good shot. Why? Because the average golfer does not have the physical strength to hit through the rough and contact the ball with the force a touring pro has.

Once in a while this shot is played by an experienced player, but usually out of great desperation. Considering the odds against ex-

#4 or #5 WOOD

MIDDLE IRON

#9 or WEDGE

ecuting a proper shot, I would readily dispense with any thought of ever using a wood from the rough.

Plan to hit an iron towards the green and then you probably have only a short pitch shot left. Get this pitch shot close enough for one putt, and your score is the same as if you had blasted that million-to-one shot onto the green and two putted.

SHOTS FROM THE DIVOT HOLES

HUMAN NATURE never helps when it comes to playing shots from the divot holes left by some inconsiderate golfer. It is human to try to pick the ball up out of the divot hole with a scooping action in the swing. In trying to "help" the ball into the air, you will hit behind the ball, or not hit it at all.

Implant in your mind this thought before you hit any shot from a divot hole: the position of your head and shoulders must remain constant. The shoulders may turn to describe the arc, but they must remain over the balance point. The head must be held steady, and the swing must be unhurried and firm.

DIVOT HOLE

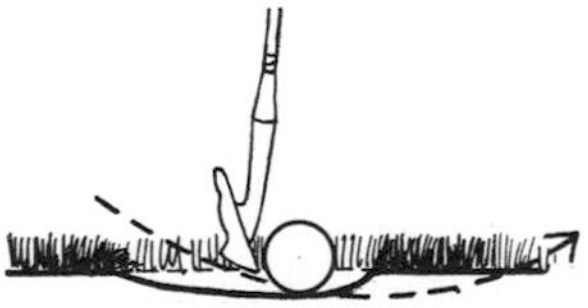

PLAYING OUT OF
A DIVOT HOLE

PLAYING FROM SOFT,
LUSH GRASS

The grip, too, must be firm, and you must consciously hit "through" each shot of this type. Too many golfers quit their swings from some sort of fear when they approach the hitting area. This is harmful to your game. Remember that it takes only a normal swing to extricate the ball from a divot hole, nothing more.

However, if the ball is lying on the side of a big divot hole you should consider how much the impact would turn either the hosel or the clubface. If the ball lies closer to your feet in a divot, you should open the clubface. If the ball lies on the far side of the divot hole, close the clubface. Just how much you would open or close the clubface would be determined by the texture of the turf, the depth of the divot hole, and the distance to the target.

PLAYING FROM LUSH FAIRWAYS

LOVELY TO look at, delightful to know, and heaven to love—but not so good for golf shots—is a very lush, verdant greensward that allows the ball to sink halfway through its diameter.

Many a shot has been missed because a golfer hit at a ball in this type of fairway thinking the ball would sail on to its target with no bad effects. This, however, is seldom the result.

Remember, if your ball is struck with fairway grass (between the clubface and the ball) it will not sail on line, nor will it have the necessary spin to give it control.

Play the ball back an inch or two inside the left heel, toward the center of your stance. Concentrate your attention on hitting an exact spot just slightly under the center of the ball. This will get the ball up with a minimum of grass to deter it from its course.

Use as much wrist action as necessary for whatever trajectory is needed to get the ball where you want it, over all hazards.

Hitting aimlessly at the ball will never produce good gold shots. But in the case of a lush fairway, you must be especially careful to contact the ball *first*.

LONG IRONS

FIRMNESS is the word for long irons. Firm grip, firm wrist action. Any attempt to relax this needed firmness will result in disaster.

Long irons are possibly the most feared shot in golf. However, they are not so difficult as you might expect. If you swing with composure, hold the club firmly, and be positive in the stroke, the long iron shots can produce many low scores.

The stance for long irons is slightly wider than for middle iron shots but narrower than with woods. The longer shafts will allow a much wider turn of the shoulders in the backswing. A firm left arm and wrists will give control at the top of the swing. This is where most golfers let themselves get out of balance, and where most long iron shots are missed.

Consciously hit through all long iron shots. Even a long iron punch-shot has a somewhat longer follow-through.

Be brave with this shot; fear can cause more misses than any other factor.

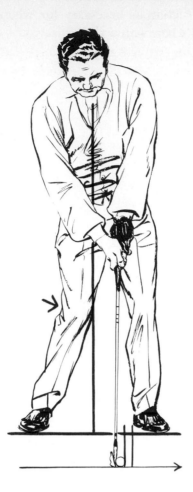

THE MIDDLE IRONS

THE ILLUSTRATION featured here shows how important is the position of the hands at the address point. Note that the hands are advanced slightly toward the hole or object. This positioning aids a downward stroke to the shot, which imparts the necessary spin to control the ball in flight. If the hands were positioned farther back they would induce a scooping motion in the swing and produce a poor shot. Hitting behind the ball is often caused by this type of hand positioning.

Note the position of the ball in relation to the feet. It is just slightly inside a perpendicular line off the left heel in relation to the intended line of flight. While this may appear to be a bit forward, remember that when the weight is shifted back to the left side, the apogee of the swing shifts forward.

The right knee is slightly kinked in toward the left, as in practically all golf shots, because the right hand is lower on the shaft. This produces a lower right shoulder and a right knee bent slightly more than the right. This is imperative if one expects to maintain balance throughout the golf swing.

THE MIDDLE IRON BACKSWING

BY FAR the easiest club to use is the number five iron. It has enough loft on the clubface to get a fairly high trajectory but at the same time is not for great distance. In this regard, you will be fairly composed while swinging it and consequently hit a fairly decent shot most of the time.

In the backswing of this middle iron, note that the hands have just about reached shoulder height. At this point you have the hands holding the club firmly but not tightly and relaxed but not loose. The clubface is square to slightly closed and the shaft points toward the objective.

The shoulders have turned as far away as possible, and the back of the golfer illustrated here has turned to face the hole or green.

This nice turn is possible because the golfer has the knees bent and is in perfect balance.

The wrists are fully cocked, as in all full shots, and the stance is slightly open to allow the clubhead to travel back from the ball slightly outside the line of flight. Then the downswing will be slightly outside-in and produce the desired cut or spin across the ball to give it the necessary controlled flight and subsequent stopping action when it hits the green.

It is not necessary to force any shot in the bag, and it is unforgivable to force an iron shot. There is no prize for getting more distance with an iron. Remember, irons are for accuracy. You have nine of them for the different distances required; use the right club and swing with the proper swing.

PLAYING THE SHORT IRONS

IN THE scoring zone, from 150 yards to the flag, control is the most important factor.

Since the shorter irons have shorter shafts, you will naturally be swinging somewhat shorter. This will make your swing a bit more upright, which is what you need.

Prime consideration should be given to the angle of the club across the ball. Most short shots call for a cut across from outside in, as in a slice. The shorter the iron, the more difficult it will be to slice the ball. This is why a cut across the ball is recommended. The cut will put the proper backspin on the shot and not let the ball fly off line. Just the opposite from the long shots, the cut across will aggravate the slice, due to the loft on the club, i.e., the angle of attack.

The shorter the club, the less you will have to shift your weight.

Naturally, the shorter the shot, the more accurate you will have to be, and the less margin for error you can afford.

In short irons the hands are advanced forward toward the hole. This promotes hitting down on the ball. This downward stroke gives the ball the desired backspin. It also precludes scooping the ball and hitting behind it, both of which cause misses or half-misses.

For shots from soft turf, consider the extra roll the ball is sure to have. From tight lies remember to keep that left shoulder high and use minimal wrist action.

SHORT IRONS
FROM WET GROUNDS

We<small>T ground</small> can produce harmful effects on the spin of a golf ball and ruin chances of a good shot. Wet ground has essentially the same dynamic effect on a ball that grass and clover have; it removes or lessens the spin, which in turn lessens control.

To improve your chances of a good shot, make certain you hit the ball first, just below center, and let the club travel through the hitting area, descending into the wet ground *after* the ball is away in flight.

Be sure that the left shoulder remains in its address position, high. Minimize wrist action throughout the swing and leave most of the weight on the left side.

If rules permit wiping the ball, by all means do so. A wet ball struck by a wet clubface can have little spin. And a ball without spin is a shot without control.

HIGH GRASS AND CLOVER

MANY SHOTS from high grass never get out of the rough, and few golfers realize that grass can entangle a club neck (hosel) and foul it up just as water grass fouls up the spinning propeller of an outboard motor.

When faced with a shot from high grass, study the amount and length of the grass. If the grass is thin and not too high, hit with a slightly open clubface. Remember that the grass will remove the spin from the shot, so aim slightly to the left.

When the grass is high and deep, firm up your grip, reconcile yourself to a very upright swing, and strike the ball as vertical a blow as possible. Open the clubface wide so that it becomes square at impact. Otherwise, the grass will wrap around the hosel and close the clubface, resulting in a missed shot.

Clover is the bane of all good golfers; they like to hit shots crisply so the ball will spin properly, hit the green, and stick. But when faced with a clover lie a good golfer realizes that he must hit with as little

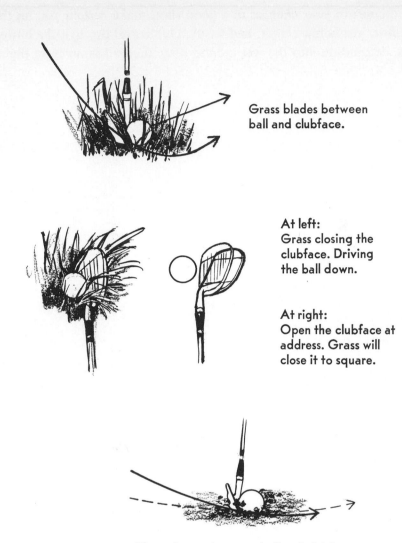

Grass blades between ball and clubface.

At left:
Grass closing the clubface. Driving the ball down.

At right:
Open the clubface at address. Grass will close it to square.

Clover leaves between ball and clubface.

clover between the blade and ball as possible. A very upright swing is a favorite method used by top golfers. The most practical attack is to align your stance absolutely square to the intended line of flight, square your shoulders and hips and take the clubface squarely away from the ball and back into the hitting area. In this way, at least the ball will have no off-line flight. Even though it will roll more than a crisp shot, you will allow for this contingency and play the shot short of the green and let it roll on to the pin.

SHORT IRONS
FROM HIGH, DEEP ROUGH

Wㅟᴇɴ ʏᴏᴜʀ ball lies in high, deep rough, check the amount of grass under and over the ball to determine the position of the clubface just prior to impact. If the ball is low in high grass, the grass will wrap around the hosel and shut the clubface before and at impact, sending the ball to the left of the objective. For a shot of this nature, open the clubface as much as forty-five degrees, depending on the length of the grass. If the ball is resting on the top portion of the high rough, set the left shoulder in a steady, high position. Square the clubface to the intended line of flight, for the grass, in relation to the ball, is not long enough to wrap itself around the hosel and close the clubface. A normal arc may be employed for this type of shot.

SHORT SHOTS—DEEP ROUGH

Wᴀᴛᴄʜɪɴɢ Johnny Pott play a ball from just over the green in a practice round of the Western Open, I saw a man with an unbelievable touch.

His second shot had carried the green and rested in very high grass on the mound of a bunker guarding the green. He was about ten feet off the "froghair" and about fifty feet from the flag. What made the shot even more difficult was the downhill slope all the way from the top of the mound to the flag.

Johnny took a wedge and softly lobbed the ball onto the green, just enough to hit the "froghair." The ball seemed about to stop ten yards short, but kept rolling until it rimmed the cup for a "gimmie" putt.

This delicate shot can be yours if you study for a moment what you need to get out of the high grass and on to the green. First, you surely do not want to hit the shot hard. Hit with a smooth stroke. Keep the hands ahead of the club, the knees flexed as much as possible, and restrict the pivot altogether. Hit the ball first, use an upright swing, and have little or no concern for a follow-through. Try to hit the ball without unbreaking the wrists. This will preclude your hitting a lot of grass between the blade and the ball.

Foremost in your mind should be the distance you need. Never think of "how" to hit it; at this point your thought must be "where" to hit the ball.

SHORT IRONS
FROM SHORT ROUGH

A POPULAR misconception of the average golfer is that any ball from any rough must be extricated by a scooping shot. A likely result is a falling back on the right side in an attempt to pick the ball into the air. Actually the opposite holds true. The ball should be struck a sharp or soft descending blow, depending on the result you want. Make certain the club contacts the ball first. Remember to remove all loose impediments from around the ball. The rules of golf penalize you if the ball should move under these circumstances, so be sure the loose impediments are not touching the ball.

SHORT IRONS INTO THE WIND

When PLAYING the short irons into the wind, it is wise to consider the angle at which your clubface usually crosses the ball. This angle of attack is important because any shot hit into the wind will react more violently if it is hit into a high trajectory. Since short irons usually go high and have less thrust, they are more prone to be affected by the headwind.

Consider, too, the distance lost by the headwind, and you will realize that you must use more club than in normal, windless conditions.

If you usually "cut" your short irons, such as slicing the shot, you must use at least two clubs more for a shot into the wind. If you draw or hook most golf shots, you would still have to hit at least one club more for a shot into the wind.

There are two other factors to be considered. Adjust the position of the ball back toward the rear foot and hold the hands ahead of the ball. This promotes a punch-type shot and will keep the ball a bit lower into the wind.

The second consideration, and the more important one, is to aim to the side of the target. Either a slice or a hook will be curving more than usual into a headwind. Make these adjustments physically and mentally *before* starting the swing.

SHORT IRONS—TIGHT LIES

Possibly the most delicate shot in the bag is the one off hard ground, close to the green. Without exception, this shot can cause more misses than a bad temper. However, it need not be as tough as most golfers make it. The first consideration is to take heart; confidence makes all the difference.

The key to success in making this shot is keeping the body as motionless as possible, leaving about sixty per cent of the weight on the left foot and using a minimum amount of wrist action, keeping the arc flat as in a long putt. Sloppy wrist action here will make the shot far more difficult. Make sure the left shoulder is high; this is another key factor to control. Try to pinch the ball by striking it just before you hit the hard ground and continue on with the stroke as if you must hit through.

Selection of the club will depend on the needed loft of the shot. Should there be a mound or other obstacle in your line, use a

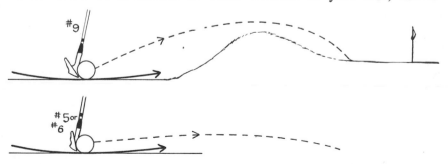

TIGHT LIES ON HARD GROUND CLOSE TO THE GREEN

number nine or ten iron. Keep the hands forward of the clubhead at address and try to keep the left hand moving toward the hole at all times. The "bump" stroke is desirable here. When the ground is fairly level don't risk a missed shot with a highly lofted club; use a number five or six iron instead.

Consider the circumstances surrounding each shot, and if you feel uneasy, always use a club with little loft. Then if you miss the shot there will be less penalty to pay.

BALL ON HIGH TUFTED GRASS

On VERY FEW courses in the world will you find high-tufted grass. However, you may sometimes find an isolated patch of this type of grass, and you should know how to extricate the ball with a good shot. Be especially careful about the left shoulder position. Keep it high, use it as an axis of the swing, and try to visualize hitting the ball just below the center. This will preclude the scooping move that sometimes accompanies a hit from grass. Never try to sweep the ball off unless the tufted grass is very heavy and able to withstand the strike of the blade. Lightly tufted grass, especially when there is grass behind the ball, will sometimes part and cause

BALL ON TUFTED GRASS

EXCEPTION

the ball to fall below its position at address. Use the sweeping stroke only when the ball sits on top of heavily tufted grass and always carry the left shoulder high.

THE EXCEPTION

Clumps of very thick tufts are frequently seen on golf courses near sandy areas. These isolated tufts can mean a lost stroke if your ball rests behind one. There is no shot in the bag that will enable a golf shot to be hit properly against the ball because of the obstinate thickness of the turf. A shot to the side is the only possible one. When executing this shot, make certain you do not hit the ball too hard or too short, for this may create other problems Decide first where you want the ball to go, think of the distance involved, and then hit the shot to that spot. Aimlessly hitting such a shot can very often mean another wasted stroke.

THE USE OF
A VERTICAL BACKSWING

WHILE THE illustration on page 72 may look improbable to you, it actually did occur when the author was playing a round of golf with the illustrator. A long drive on a dog-leg hole to the right was hit straight down the middle, and a slight hook took it into the rough.

A small sapling was approximately fifteen inches behind the ball, in the line of the normal backswing. The ball rested an inch in front of a smaller sapling. A look at this situation might make a player take a penalty stroke and drop the ball two club lengths away, as permitted in the U.S. Golf Association Rules of Golf. However, a bit of thinking and some odd swinging made this shot almost easy.

First consider the backswing. It is not unusual that circumstances

CLUBFACE CLOSES TO SQUARE

will hinder your backstroke, so be prepared for the possibility with a little practice. Lift the club straight up from the ball, turning the shoulders to the normal top-of-the-swing position, and then return the weight to the left side and go through the usual motion of hitting the ball. This will usually produce a fine shot.

In this particular situation, the smaller sapling near the ball presented another problem. The hosel hit the sapling and caused the clubface to turn just before impact. From the illustration insert you can see that the clubface had been held wide open. Since the sapling held the club back a bit and allowed the face to turn shut, this made it square with the ball at impact.

There also happened to be a tree in the line to the pin, so the shot had to be played to the center of the green instead of directly to the pin. However, from this seemingly impossible situation, the shot was executed very simply.

THE WHAT, WHEN, WHERE,
AND HOW OF SIDEHILL LIES

WHILE NOTHING can take the place of continual practice, you should know how to recognize a situation that could lead to a poor golf shot and learn to make the proper corrections *before* the miss.

For an uphill lie (one in which the ball and your feet are on the same level but the slope of the hill makes your aim high) play the ball back towards the center of the stance and use at least one club longer than you would for the same distance on a flat lie. Aim to the right of the green, for you will be inclined to pull the shot to the left.

For a downhill lie, aim to the left and use one club longer; the slicing ball will not have the distance that a pulled or hooked shot would have. The ball should be played toward the right of center of the stance.

The same applies if the ball is on a sidehill lie, at a level lower than your feet. Bend the knees more to sit down closer to the ball, back on your heels, to permit the proper balance for this unusual shot.

If the ball is above your feet in a sidehill lie, you will have to aim to the right of the green and grip the club shorter, for the ball will be closer to the center of your arc and your regular length club will be too long. Compensate for this adjusted length by using one club longer. Weight balance should be slightly forward toward the toes so that you do not fall backward while swinging.

Look for the general slope of the terrain before hitting any shot on a hilly golf course. Many slopes can be deceiving, and study of the art of playing the hills will bring a lower score.

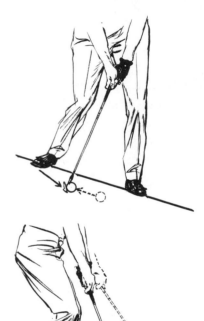

THE FLIP-SHOT

No shot has ever given me more satisfaction than the flip-shot. This must be done with the most highly lofted club in the bag. It should be practiced at every opportunity, for you should be capable of producing it when you need it. It calls for a wide-open clubface, a maximum amount of wrist action, and a cut across the ball more pronounced than at any other time.

A very weak grip is also very important. Turn the hands counterclockwise so that they will not turn the clubface closed through the hitting area. Use an open stance to promote the cutting action needed for the spin. You will be delighted to see how high a ball can ride and how little distance you can get with a full swing. The distance you need will determine just how much you open the clubface and the amount of velocity you will use, through the ball.

Never try this shot off hard ground, for the club must completely pass under the ball; from hard ground you will invariably hit somewhere below center but never completely under the ball, resulting in a ruined shot and a damaged golf ball.

THE SHORT CHIP SHOT

Take a moment to study the margin for error in all golf shots and you are struck with the vast differences between woods and very short irons. For comparison, consider a tee shot. It can very easily travel off line twenty yards and still be in the fairway in good position. Conversely, hit a short chip shot twenty yards off line and you'd have to call for the Civil Air Patrol to find you.

In the wood shot, a huge body turn with arms swinging and great clubhead speed can produce a good chance for error. In the little chip shot, too often the golfer tries to hit the shot with a full swing.

The swing should be short. This is understandable; the shot is short. The ball is played as far back toward the center of the stance as practicable (this still puts it inside the left heel only an inch or two but the turned-out position of the left foot makes it appear off the right foot). Keep the hands close to the body and the knees bent as much as possible. Sitting 'way down to the ball will aid in "locking up" the swing. The open stance allows the clubhead to travel out and across the line of flight. This eliminates much of the overspin and will give more consistently good chip shots.

Beware of "flipping" the wrists at the ball. Turn the shoulders to produce the short shot; let the wrists be fully cocked as soon as you take the club back, and never try to hit with the wrists after that. Just let the feel come from the shoulders and fingertips.

CHIP BACK TO SAFETY

As THE illustration indicates, we have selected a route away from the pin instead of trying an almost impossible shot to the flag.

Thinking of how far we want the ball to travel in the air and on the ground, we make a judicious club selection. If we have to get the ball over high turf and/or weeds and shrubbery, we would use a wedge. Should the grass be just normal height rough, we would take a somewhat less lofted club, say a number seven or eight iron.

When playing away from the ultimate object, the important thing is not to waste still another stroke by hitting the wrong club or hitting the ball a distance that would put you once again in a position of compromise.

Watch your weight shifting; if the center of the swing moves off the ball, the shot could easily be missed.

FROM THE SAND TRAP

Ask the average golfer if he likes to play sand shots and chances are he will say no. Then ask him if he ever practiced the sand-trap shot and you may be certain he hasn't. Watch the tournament greats practice, and you'll always see the practice sand trap occupied by one of the better players. You cannot expect to recóver well from the traps if you have not given time to practicing the shot.

Two general types of trap shots exist, the ball atop the sand and the buried ball. Neither one is really difficult if you think of the solutions.

While it is against the rules of golf to test the texture of sand, you would be wise to learn to do this while taking your stance. Merely walking up to the ball in sand and hitting at it will never prove effective. You must get a firm footing. You are swinging the club and your weight will push your feet deeper into the sand and you will miss the shot. Get those feet deeply imbedded first. An open stance is usually desired in sand.

For the shot atop the sand you will be using an open clubface and taking a bit of sand behind the ball. This will give you a good cutting action on the ball, and the backspin will stop the ball within reasonable distance. The amount of sand you take should be determined by the texture of the sand. Generally speaking, if the sand is soft and dry (fine) you will get less distance. Practice with this to find out just how much. With wet and/or coarse sand you will have to hit with less power. Usually a ball will "fly" out of wet, packed sand.

With a buried ball you should consider that on impact the sand will open the clubface no matter how firmly you grip the club. The clubface should be closed for this shot. Above all else, hit through every sand shot with as smooth and unhurried a swing as possible.

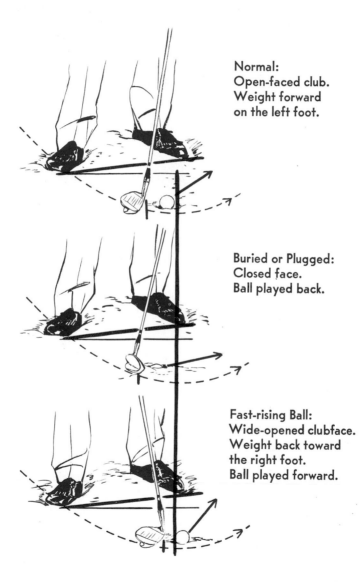

Normal:
Open-faced club.
Weight forward
on the left foot.

Buried or Plugged:
Closed face.
Ball played back.

Fast-rising Ball:
Wide-opened clubface.
Weight back toward
the right foot.
Ball played forward.

VARIOUS LIES IN THE SAND TRAP

For MOST trap shots hit from one to two inches behind the ball. Practice this so that you'll be familiar with how much swing you'll need for so much distance.

The illustration shows a ball in the sand trap approximately twenty feet from the flag. The question is whether the ball should be chipped out or blasted out.

If you have the sensitive touch of a brain surgeon, I'd say chip it out; but of all the great golfers in the world, I have seen only two who would chance a chip shot from the trap. It is one that must be played with a very firm left side, no weight shift and no flipping of wrists. There can be no margin for error here. Miss the ball one eighth of an inch and you have missed the shot. This applies to either the top or bottom of the spot where the ball should be struck. The follow-through should not be considered in a shot as short as this one. Practice it a

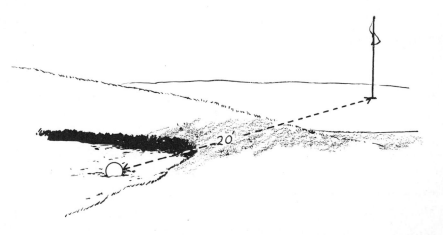

bit before you ever try it in actual play. The pressure of playing a match or tournament brings double trouble. Blasting is better.

Blasting a ball from either a clean lie or buried lie has been proved the best method of extricating a ball from the sand trap. It is not a shot that requires the greatest accuracy to get out and on the green. Of course, accuracy is better, but consider the sand your safety cushion, permitting you to make a slight mistake.

A twenty-foot blast is an abbreviated shot. Grip the club, 'way down on the bottom of the grip. Open the stance and flex the knees as much as possible. Take the club back smoothly, unhurried and not too far. Leave the weight on the left side and do not shift it at all. Have the wrists half-cocked at address and never try to uncock them in the swing. Let them unleash whatever force they will with no conscious effort on your part.

THE EXPLOSION SHOT FROM TURF

IT DOES NOT necessarily hold that all explosion shots should be made from the sand traps. Many times you will see a tournament player take a full shot with a wedge from a few yards off the green. This is usually done when the ball is in a poor lie or partially buried in the ground. Stretch your imagination to the point that you visualize the clubface dishing up a divot to the green. This not only takes your mind off the ball but allows you full concentration on the actual job you should be doing, throwing the turf up to the green with your wedge.

The distance to the pin will determine just how hard you should swing, how much turf you will take, and the length of your backswing. Many golfing greats use all three considerations; others do it with less sand and/or turf between the ball and the blade.

An open clubface can almost be a distance-determining factor. Should the lie be such that you can contact the ball first, use a wide-open clubface and watch the ball sail high. It will land from a vertical trajectory and have little if any roll.

THOSE SILLY SLOPES

GOLF might be played better if all fairways were flat, all greens were slightly pitched towards the oncoming golfer, and there were no undulations to send the rolling ball careening offsides. However, we probably would not be satisfied without the challenges that every round brings.

In this illustration we see three types of shots to be executed. The highest slope looks like a mountainside. Remember also the very short run to the flag once you are on top. A very delicate wedge shot is called for. Use a wide-open clubface, an open stance, and a swing far outside-in. The ball must be played just to clear the top of the mound. As indicated, the short slope to the flag will take care of whatever momentum the ball still has.

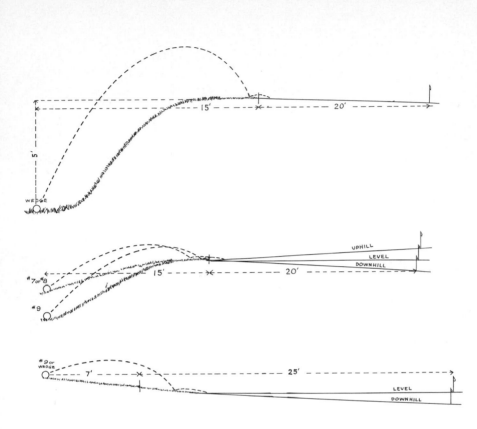

The second shot requires almost as much dexterity. Here we must choose a chipping club. A number seven or eight iron would give enough loft to land the ball on the "froghair" at the green's edge and still have enough force to carry on to the green's surface. The first bounce should take your ball to the putting surface, and the ball should have little overspin. Play the ball to the green's edge, not to the flag.

The third shot calls for a wedge or a number nine iron. Again the ball should be played off the left heel, with an open stance and an open clubface. Pick a spot halfway through the "froghair," and the ball should lose its forward thrust about the time it reaches the putting surface. At this time the green slope will carry the ball all the way to the flag.

In all three shots shown here we must consider that the delicacy of the shot precludes a bold stroke to the flag. This is what is known as a dying shot.

The ball should lose all of its forward thrust just as it reaches the green. Then slope and unused momentum will do the rest. Of course you still must line the shot up for the break that may be an inherent part of the surface. Grip down on the shaft, as this is an abbreviated shot.

PUTTING

IT SOMETIMES seems unjust that a two-inch putt should count as heavily in scoring as a three-hundred-yard drive. Sometimes a long putt to the flag may be resting immediately adjacent to the fringe area of the green. A putter is used, of course, but it is impossible to stroke the ball from behind as you would if the ball were on the putting surface with no long grass interfering, as in this illustration.

The best way to play this shot is to play a topped putt. By stroking over the ball, you will get more overspin. Another way is to strike down

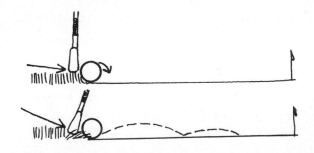

and play a hopping putt. This second type will have less control than the first, but the first one is ticklish. You will find the topped putt will roll more than the hopping putt but not so far as a solidly hit putt. Allow for this when considering the distance required to get the ball to the hole.

Few high-handicappers consider the grain in the green. All tournament greats know that if the grain is toward the hole (leaning toward the hole) the ball will roll faster. If the grain is against the direction of the putt, naturally the ball would go slower.

Another important factor in putting is the side spin on the ball. If

GRAIN GOING AWAY IS FASTER

GRAIN GOING AGAINST IS SLOWER

you stroke across the ball, the ball rolling against the grain will go much farther off line, just as a slice or hook does against the wind. This is one reason why golfing greats try to stroke their putts straight back and straight through on line.

When playing in high-humidity areas in the morning the grass is short but damp, and consequently the putts will have to be stroked harder for the distance. Around noon the grass is still short but drier and the putts would go farther. In the afternoon, putting is a problem on heavily traversed golf courses due to the play and the indentations made by golfers' shoes and scuff marks. The grass, too, is longer. While it is drier and longer, it will make for some erratic putting. All of these contingencies are to be taken into consideration when playing your putts.

Great putters invariably consider distance rather than direction when putting. One will instinctively putt in the proper direction, but it is strange how few think of distance. Of all the "sleepers" in putting we occasionally see a good player come up far short or go 'way beyond the cup. This is just plain carelessness and lack of concentration.

CLUB SELECTION
FOR DELICATE SHOTS

SELDOM IF EVER will you be faced with a shot just like the one illustrated here. But similar circumstances are not uncommon.

A look at the edge of the trap indicates that a piece of turf lies between the ball and the clubface. Ordinarily a golfer would grab a sand wedge and blast away. But let us consider the effect some wedges may have on this particular shot. There is a very well-known model of sand wedge that has a rocker-sole. This type of sole is perfect for extricating balls from sand lies. But the same sole can wreak havoc if you plan to do a little turf cutting in the downward stroke. The rocker would cause the club to bounce a bit off the turf and cut into the ball rather than the turf. In this particular situation, a pitching wedge with a knife-like leading edge would be far more practical.

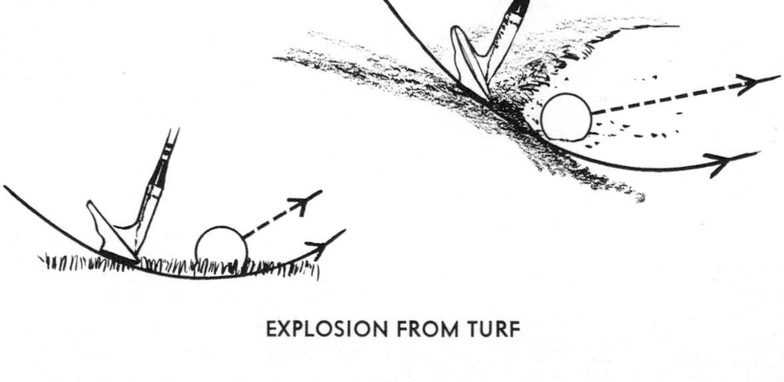

EXPLOSION FROM TURF

THE JOE KIRKWOOD, SR., HANGING LIE

For the shot over the head, a sand wedge is definitely the club to use. It has the most loft and will do the job better than any other club in the bag. When playing this shot, be sure to bend the right knee to allow the scooping motion to go through the shot with no interruption.

The venerable Joe Kirkwood, Sr., used to feature this type of shot in his trick-shot repertoire. He would place the ball on the back ledge of the trap and take a very lofted iron (such as today's wedge) and flip the ball backwards over his head and on to the green. He made many seemingly miraculous shots this way, to the great pleasure and astonishment of his audience. The illustration here shows how this is

done. While I do not suggest trying it when playing for a title or trophy, I do urge all to try it in practice. Then if the problem ever presents itself, you will not give up the ghost so quickly.

PLAYING OUT OF THE WOODS

TREES ARE lovely—and a big pest for straying golfers. Somewhere the great Walter Hagen is credited with saying that a tree is ninety percent air and ten percent solid. Although I would never dispute Sir Walter, the odds must be against me and all the golfers with whom I have played. I would suggest that trees are about sixty percent solid and forty percent air. Bark marks on my ball will attest to this.

There are many ways to play out of the woods; some are safe, some suicidal. First, be realistic. If there is a big gaping hole through the trees on line to the green or flag, by all means go for it. However, if you don't hit all your shots straight how can you possibly hope to get out on line through these trees? Reconsider; it may be possible to hit your normal slice around some trees through a bigger opening. However, you do not have to hit the green at all. Why not play the ball down the fairway as far as possible, leaving yourself an easy pitch to the green for a possible one putt.

Many a great tournament has been lost by one foolish shot on just one hole. Only in desperation should one try the improbable. If you are down in match play, if the decision hangs on the hole you are playing out of the woods on, then go for the shot.

First clean all foreign objects from around the ball. Too often a ball will be sitting on small twigs. These will invariably send a shot far off line at impact. Make certain, though, not to move the ball when you move a twig or other object. This costs a stroke by every rule in the book. In stroke play, a foolish try at getting the ball out of the woods is the worst solution.

PLAYING THE IMPROBABLE SHOTS

Should you be the unfortunate victim of a lie such as the one illustrated here, be wise enough to consider the possibility of getting the ball on to any part of the green, rather than close to the pin.

A high pitch shot with a wide-open clubface can get you on to the back of the green. A shot to the side of the green can get you on the surface, where the next shot would be a cinch. But the only possible

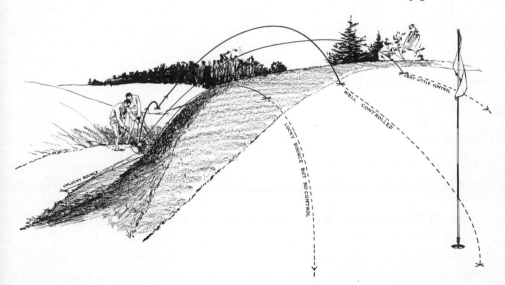

shot that would get you near the pin requires an element you should never depend on—luck.

The shot you must hit would be directed into the bank or hill of the green's approach. Next time you're out on the course waiting for the match ahead to clear the fairway, practice this shot a few times. Try it with several clubs and from several lies. If you must try this shot in a game, consider the height of the grass, as this factor will affect the roll of the shot. Figure that grass a half inch high will slow the ball down appreciably only if the ball rolls in it. One bounce through half-inch grass will not have too much effect on the distance. However, grass over an inch in height can almost stop the ball; consider carefully before making a shot into grass of such height. Grass of two inches and higher should be avoided. It would be folly to try to hit into and out of this grass with a bouncing shot.

In the first illustration, note that the angle of the clubface is quite obtuse to the normal clubface path. When faced with such a lie you have only to turn the clubface to the proper angle, grip the club normally, and swing away from the obstruction—in this illustration, the tree. Think subconsciously of the distance required and the clubface path.

The second illustration indicates another unlikely lie. However, as in the first, we must dispatch the ball with as little loss as possible. Usually the toe of the putter can be employed to wedge in the crack

and make contact with the ball. You may, of course, use any other club that will fit in and have a surface that will allow a proper stroke to send the ball off on line. The purpose of this entire lesson is to show you the many alternates that can rescue the errant shot. All it takes on your part is some advance thinking.

A very common bad break is the downhill lie, shown here. Most golfers take a flailing stroke at the ball and try to get it out anywhere. You can be more practical if you consider the degree of loft on your sand wedge; with the shaft leaning forward you have the equivalent of a two iron or putter. This may be enough loft to get the ball over the bunker or other hazard. The pitfall here is not necessarily the lie, but the manner in which you attack the problem shot. Plan the shot; don't hit aimlessly. The ball should be played off the right foot in this instance because of the downhill lie and the angle at which your clubhead will descend into the ball. No pivot or weight shift should be used. While you should consciously hit through the ball, you will find that the club will seldom if ever get far beyond the ball. It is a more upright stroke, and the vertical descending club can go on farther than the turf under the ball.

There are times when the souls of men are tried and found wanting. Look at the shot described in the illustration and you see what one golfer actually had to negotiate. First, he had a tough shot even if the ball was teed up, which it most assuredly wasn't. It was on a nasty downhill lie. From his normal stance angle, he couldn't even stand right to hit the shot, and the hill in front of him and between his ball and the pin was imposing, to say the least.

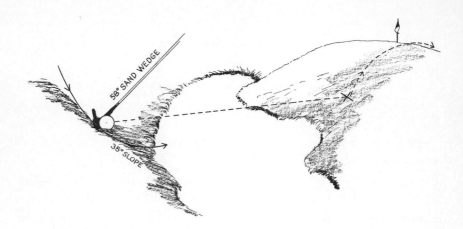

He actually had three ways to attack this problem. The easiest was to take a sand wedge (since this club has the most loft), stand to the side of the ball, and crowd the clubface over the ball. With this angle, the club became something like a number six iron, a club with which he could normally chip the shot. He should hit the ball into the bank and allow a bit more distance because of the loss of speed caused by the ball's striking the grassy bank. Consider, too, the slope of the green, and play the ball so that when the speed dies the ball will take the curve of the green.

A second way to hit the ball is back onto the back and safe side of the green. Few golfers will hit away from the hole but the wise ones often do.

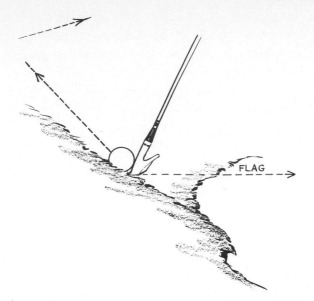

The third possibility is even more painful to the average golfer's imagination—hit the ball back on to the fairway or approach end of the green. This sacrificial shot is usually done when there is no alternative. No golfer likes to waste a stroke. But a wise player knows that one sacrificed stroke in an impossible situation will very likely save subsequent shots.

The illustration at the top shows a ball resting against a sloping bank. This is a situation with many variables, but one thing should be very obvious to the golfer: there is no way to get the ball near the pin. Plan your shot to get into the best possible position for the next stroke. Trying to hit directly to the pin would leave the ball in the hazard, waste a stroke, leave yourself another bad lie, and possibly sprain your wrists from the club impacting against the bank. Think of the shot you must make to get the ball near the hole. Play away from the bank so that the territory you hit to will be a good one, giving you a good chance to play close or possibly sink the next shot. Consider the green, the slopes, etc. Don't hit to an area where you would have a downhill shot to negotiate or a bunker to cross.

Another type of sacrificial shot is illustrated on page 94. Here we have the same downhill lie as before from which to try to get the ball

93

on the green. Playing it away from the hole affords an easier shot away and back. Consider the player who demands that his shot be in the direction of the hole. When he hits at the ball on this slope he either leaves it on the slope or hits it into the trap or hazard. But use caution when extricating yourself from this lie. Plan to hit to good, level territory. Think of the distance required to get back to fair ground; don't hit the ball back up the slope with reckless abandon.

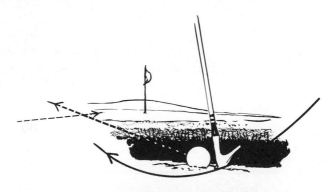

CHIP SIDEWAYS TO SAFETY

BALL AGAINST OBSTRUCTION

Should you find your ball lying against a wall, fence, or other obstruction and the rules permit no free lift, take heart; you will find that you may be able to turn this into a shot that will be the talk of the country club for some time.

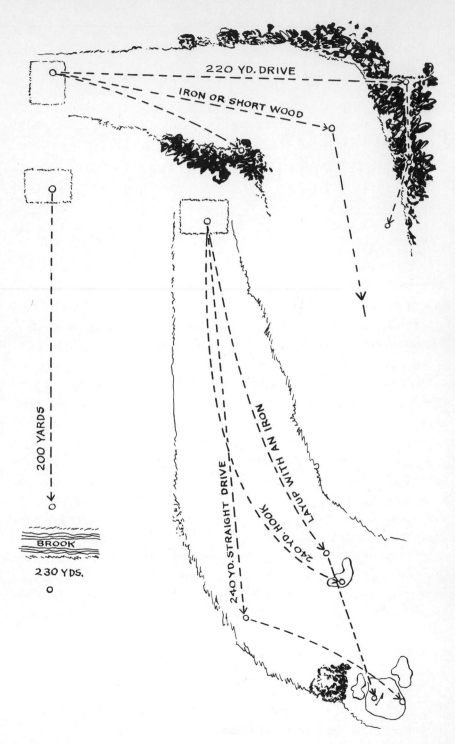

220 YD. DRIVE

IRON OR SHORT WOOD

200 YARDS

BROOK

230 YDS.

240 YD. STRAIGHT DRIVE

240 YD. HOOK

LAYUP WITH AN IRON

PLAYING LOW
UNDER THE BRANCHES

ANOTHER actual situation that arose during a match between the author and illustrator is shown in this sketch. The illustrator's drive was hit to the center of the fairway, but the slope of the fairway turned the shot to the left side, in a very difficult position for the second shot to this four-par hole. The slope of the hill, from right to left and downhill, was considerable.

The tree shown was directly in line to the flag. The trap on the right side of the green stood guard for the errant shot, as did one

on the left. Trees lined the right side of the rough to the far right.

The solution was determined by considering whether to play for a high spot over the right side of the tree with a hook, or a low shot to the right side, risking the bunker's catching the shot as it came in towards the pin. Since the downhill, sidehill lie suggested a placement of the ball back to the right foot, it was decided to play the low ball.

The green was about 155 yards away. Because of its straighter face, a number 3 iron was first selected. The shot was hit, executed perfectly, and the ball rode out to the right in a low sweeping arc and curved back into the line to the pin. It rolled over the green, and a number 4 iron was selected and hit perfectly to the center of the green.

To check with the results of a high shot we chose a number 6 iron and tried a hook over the tree and around to the green. Maximum wrist action was needed to get the ball up, but since the ball had to be played back towards the right foot, the shot couldn't climb high and fast enough to clear the tree. It actually did just nip the leaves, but that slowed the ball enough to make it stop twenty yards short of the green.

Remember to minimize the wrist action through the hitting area when playing low shots and to use as much wrist action as possible for the high shots.

Remember, too, for the sidehill and downhill lie, the position of the ball should be adjusted to the center or back of center of the stance.

DOWNHILL LIE
LEFT FOOT LOWER

CLOSED FACE

USING THE CLUB UPSIDE DOWN

THIS ILLUSTRATION shows the most commonly used alternate in golf. Frequently a right-hand shot is impossible. In such cases, by merely turning an iron upside down, you can make the stroke towards the green with a lefthanded swing.

Since the clubfaces have different angles or lofts, you should consider using a club with as little loft as possible. Also remember, however, that a club with the least loft has the narrowest blade face, which diminishes your hitting area. I find that a number six or seven iron will produce the best shots. You must be aware of the change in direction, since the loft of the club will angle the ball to the right of the pin. Play the ball back toward the left foot (which is converse), and be sure to keep your head steady over the ball. The greatest wrecker of this shot is fear. A restriction of the weight shifting is also desirable, for any excess motion can help ruin the shot. Visualize the line to the object (green or fairway), and then think only of the distance you'll need.

THE KNEELING SHOT

IF THERE is one shot in my trick-shot repertoire that delights an audience, it is the kneeling drive. For any distance from 180 to 230 yards, this shot is amazingly simple. In fact, on two occasions I have rimmed the cup from tees over two hundred yards away using the kneeling stance.

There are times when a golfer may use this shot to advantage—under the spreading branches of a tree, for example. If the branches prevent a good backswing, use this shot. At first you will hit all shots behind the ball, but with practice you will find it very simple just to drop to your knees and hit the ball with any club in your bag.

Playing with an executive, John E. Farrell, in New Jersey a few years ago, I found this very dignified man under a tree on his knees. He hit the ball out to the fairway from an almost impossible lie. He grinned up at me and said, "I saw you do it, so I tried."

If you must use an iron from the knees, remember that the angle of the blade will cause the ball to hook—the more loft, the more hook.

THE DANGERS OF ROOTS AND ROCKS

LARGE TREES have large roots; sometimes small trees have large roots; and all can be trouble to a golfer.

When your ball comes to rest near a tree, check to see if there are any partially submerged roots near the ball. If you suspect some but do not see them, probe around the ball with a tee.

There have been many instances recorded where a golfer will strike a very good shot from near a tree and as the club descended through the impact area it would strike a root and turn the club face into the ball or abruptly stop the club. This can cause a sprained wrist, a broken bone, a broken clubshaft—and last but not least a lost stroke.

Rocks can cause the same trouble. A buried rock is not uncommon on golf courses, especially in the northern latitudes when the changes of weather and temperature bring many boulders to the surface each spring. Check carefully if you suspect hidden or half-hidden rocks or roots.

THE CYCLE:
FEEL, ACCURACY, SCORING

IT WOULD be folly indeed for anyone to take a golf lesson, dash out to the golf course, and try to implement what was digested on the lesson tee. Your muscles must become accustomed to a new action or position before it will "feel" right. And you will need even more practice before it works right.

Never delude yourself about your chances of hitting shot after shot just right. It has been said that golf is a game of misses; the person who misses the shots just a little will be better off than one who misses them completely. Realize that you are not really capable of hitting every shot perfectly. With this knowledge you may go out and marvel at the many actual good shots you hit. Worrying about the missed shots will not produce anything but more misses.

Consider the many margins for error, the many, many ways to miss a golf shot and you'll probably wind up by forgetting the score-card altogether, which may be the only way to enjoy the game. I have long subscribed to the theory that if you play golf for fun and you get livid with rage on missing a shot, forget the game, you are its servant and the game affords you no fun. However, you can reconcile yourself to one indisputable fact. When the blood rushes to the brain, as it does when we get angry, the chances of your hitting any shot will be too remote to consider.

After each lesson, go out and work the new position or action until it begins to feel right. After you get the feel, you will soon be amazed to see the accuracy begin to strike a consistent pattern of behavior. From this evolves a pattern of consistent scoring. The cycle is obvious: from practice comes the right feel, from the feel comes accuracy, and from accuracy come low scores.

A WORD ABOUT "SWINGWEIGHT"

I F THERE is one psychological factor that has ruined the too studious golfer, it is "swingweight." This is merely a scale that shows the weight or feel of a club in relation to the grip handle and the clubhead. A dime on top of a clubhead can change the swingweight one point.

However, swingweight cannot be felt in degrees of one or two points. It would take at least three points of the swingweight scale for any appreciable change of feel to be recognized, even by top professionals.

Swingweight becomes important when your professional is measuring you up for a set of golf clubs. He will use the swingweight scale to determine the weight (overall) you need. The shaft length, the swingweight, the size of the grip, and the loft and lie of the club are factors your pro knows must be taken into consideration.

THE FUN OF GOLF

G OLF is to be played for fun and relaxation. A number of missed shots, even putts, should not spoil your enjoyment of the game.

Know your true capacity and play well within it. Since forcing a shot is the most common error of the average golfer, we stress very strongly that you make it a firm rule never to go beyond your ability. No professional golfer tries the impossible.

Be patient when taking lessons, and never take advice from someone who knows very little about the fundamentals. Play with the equipment recommended by your PGA professional. Most of all, learn to laugh at yourself and you'll find new horizons of happiness on the golf course.

CONCLUDING THOUGHTS

W HILE ETIQUETTE has nothing directly to do with the mechanics of a golf swing, it can, nonetheless, affect your game when any of the following are violated.

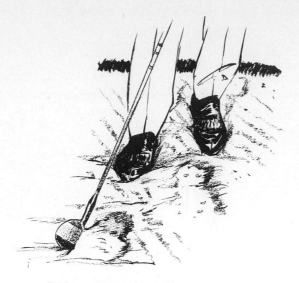

SMOOTH SAND AFTER PLAYING

REPLACE DIVOT

REPAIR BALL MARKS ON GREEN

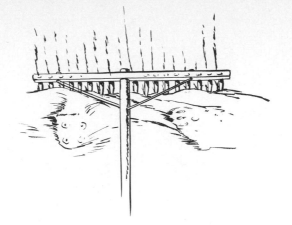

RAKE SAND AFTER PLAYING

The golden rule should apply in golf. There are rules of etiquette spelled out very plainly. In fact, the U. S. Golf Association has a series of cartoons, available to member clubs, showing how the etiquette of golf is often violated and how simple it is to correct these bad habits. Many annoyances result when any golfer or group of golfers fail to consider others on the course. Do you consider the foursome ahead of you inconsiderate if they completely ignore their slow rate of play and the other players behind them? Standing on the green to add the score is another inconsiderate item.

Not many golfers are pleased to see their ball come to rest in a big divot hole. But these same golfers seldom replace their divots. Do you like to have your errant shot wind up in a sand trap? Of course not. But when it does, wouldn't it be far nicer if it just wound up on a flat surface, not in some inconsiderate golfer's footprint?

While annoyance may not affect your golf swing, it will have a profound effect on your disposition. This in turn will make you more prone to miss shots. There is a relation between playing a pleasing round of golf with agreeable companions in circumstances conducive to mental and physical relaxation, and playing well.

THINK

THERE IS one thing certain about golf. It is a thinking game. Those who play it well, who play it well consistently, think. They think before selecting a club, they think before approaching the shot. They know from experience that thinking *after* the ball has been hit is absolutely foolhardy.

They think the shot out thoroughly before swinging at the ball. After the thinking period a good golfer concentrates only on a solid hit from a smoothly executed swing.

The questions you must ask yourself while approaching the ball are:

- Is it a straight-away shot?
- Is it a complicated shot?
- How do I play this shot?
- Why should I play it this way instead of another?
- Is there an alternate route?
- What are the conditions that necessitate my playing it this way?

Study all factors as you approach the ball. Experience will teach you to do this subconsciously and you will take little if any more time than the player who plays without thinking.

Be completely realistic about the results you can expect from each shot. Play within your capacity at all times. If you choose to take a bold gamble, however, be prepared for the worst while hoping for the best.